STOKE-ON-TRENT
A Pictorial History

East Vale from the top of St James' Church, *c.*1912.

STOKE-ON-TRENT
A Pictorial History

Alan Taylor

Phillimore

1995

Published by
PHILLIMORE & CO. LTD.
Shopwyke Manor Barn, Chichester, West Sussex

ISBN 0 85033 968 5

Printed and bound in Great Britain by
BIDDLES LTD.
Guildford, Surrey

For Jan, Josh and Sam

List of Illustrations

Frontispiece: East Vale, *c.*1912

Acknowledgements

I would like to thank all those who have helped me with this book. In particular, I would like to give special thanks to Liz Salmon, Pat Halfpenny, Bill Klemperer, Sarah Macdonald, Ian Lawley and Janet Dugdale of the City Museum and Art Gallery, Stoke-on-Trent; Teresa Smith for assistance with picture research; Judith Billing for her word-processing skills and patience with my handwriting; Richard Weston for photographic copywork; Robert Downie for information; Ray Johnson for permission to use images 26, 59, 60; the North Staffordshire Miners' Wives Action Group for permission to use image 66. The paintings by Brown, Pratt and Constable are reproduced from the collection of the City Museum and Art Gallery, Stoke-on-Trent. The portrait of Wedgwood is reproduced by kind permission of the Trustees of the Wedgwood Museum, and illustration 101 is reproduced by permission of Quality Learning Services, Education Department, Staffordshire County Council. Illustration 130, the photograph of Meir Aerodrome, is reproduced by permission of John Martin, Staffordshire, Ltd.

Introduction

Stoke-on-Trent is the heart of the North Staffordshire Potteries. The city emerged in 1910 with the federation of not five, as Arnold Bennett had us believe, but six towns: Burslem, Fenton, Hanley, Longton, Stoke and Tunstall. The reputation of the pottery manufacturers has spread worldwide, but the city's name is not built on ceramics alone; the likes of Arnold Bennett, Oliver Lodge, Reginald Mitchell and Stanley Matthews have contributed to the development of the arts, engineering and sport.

Various of the towns have claimed precedence over the rest. Historically Burslem and Fenton can be traced back to manors mentioned in Domesday Book, although habitation of the wider area dates from much earlier. Small flint tools and butchered animal bones suggest that the earliest inhabitants were in the area some 10,000 years ago. Ironically, the heavy and poorly drained clay soils were unfit for cultivation and failed to provide for the Neolithic settlers in the way in which they have provided for their more modern counterparts. The area is also poor in surviving burial sites of the period, the nearest being the Bridestones. This again would suggest a poorly populated area. Celtic and Old English place-names give some indication of habitation patterns. Penkhull, which remained an important village until the 19th century, suggests a hilltop settlement, possibly a fort. Stoke itself is derived from the Old English for a holy place. Domesday Book does not mention a village at Stoke but does record the existence of a church. Evidence exists to suggest a medieval moated site adjacent to the original church. It would appear that this ancient holy site served the neighbouring village of Penkhull.

The manors of Hanley, Fenton Vivian, Fenton Culvert, Thursfield in Wolstanton (from which Tunstall's manorial origins may be drawn), Burslem, Longton, Penkhull (from which Stoke was to emerge) and Newcastle-under-Lyme, developed between the time of the Norman Conquest and the late 13th century. Domesday Book refers to Penkhull, Burslem, Thursfield and Fenton. Tunstall was established as a manor held by Aline and Engenulph de Gresley by *c.*1200. Stoke only began to emerge as a town due to the arrival of the Derby and Uttoxeter to Newcastle turnpike road and the Trent and Mersey Canal in the latter half of the 18th century. Until then only the church and a scattering of houses, mostly associated with the church, were to be found in the area.

During the late 18th and early 19th centuries, the townships emerged in something like their modern form. A large proportion of the area came under the jurisdiction of the manor of Newcastle, and Poor Law administration for Hanley, Fenton, Longton and Stoke was undertaken by the parish of Stoke-on-Trent. Tunstall and Burslem were administered by the parish of Wolstanton. During this period the pottery industry was developing and its reputation was spreading. It became apparent that a unified, corporate development of the six towns was necessary if the industry was to continue to expand.

Civic pride became an important issue during the 19th century. During the first half of the century each of the six towns appointed local improvement commissioners responsible to a greater or lesser degree for areas such as provision of lighting, street improvements and so on. Following local government reform in the middle years of that century, each town had a local board of health with powers expanded from the times of the improvement commissioners. Plans for a large board of health covering Stoke parish (the area south of Burslem and east of Newcastle-under-Lyme, some 12,000 acres of land inhabited by over 55,000 people) were dropped as a result of strong local opposition. As a consequence, Stoke retained its local board of health until 1874 when it became a borough. Hanley, Longton and Burslem became boroughs in 1857, 1865 and 1878 respectively. Fenton and Tunstall were created urban districts in 1894. This civic structure remained largely unchanged until 1910 when the County Borough of Stoke-on-Trent was formed.

The late-Victorian civic pride of each of the towns was expressed through the market halls and town halls. The importance of these buildings as a focal point can be seen in the uses to which they were often put. The original town hall in Stoke housed the market and by 1829 was also home to the fire engine. The later and present town hall, recently extended and renamed the Civic Centre, accommodated the market, the Athenaeum, the police force, the fire engine and the court room. The original town hall in Hanley was opened in 1845, but the offices were relocated to the former *Queen's Hotel* in 1884. The importance of this site was emphasised with the addition of the Victoria Hall to the rear of the building during 1887 and 1888.

The parish of Stoke-on-Trent is one of antiquity. A church existed in the area before 1086, at which time the parish encompassed Bagnall, Bucknall, Burslem, Clayton, Fenton, Hanley, Lane End, Newcastle, Norton-in-the-Moors, Seabridge and Whitmore. The parish was granted six chapels of ease during the Middle Ages, but it was not until 1807 that five rectories were created. During the Victorian period the parish was divided into smaller units: Longton (1839), Hartshill (1842), Shelton (1843), Penkhull and Trent Vale (1844), Northwood, Hanley and Wellington, Hanley (1845), Fenton (1860), Hanley St John (1891) and Shelton St Jude (1895). Tunstall formed a part of the parish of Wolstanton.

The present church at Stoke dates from between 1826 and 1829 and is a typical example of the Church Commissioners' work. Of the 13th-century building, only two arches and two responds survive; these were re-erected close to the present structure in 1887. However, this earlier church was by no means the most significant religious building in the area. On a plot adjacent to what is now a housing estate, the site of Hulton Abbey was once a remote area. The abbey was established in 1219 by the Cistercian Order and was granted land by its benefactor Henry of Audley. The monks' main income was derived from a huge flock of sheep and the production of wool. The house, however, was never wealthy, particularly when compared to other Cistercian establishments elsewhere in the county. The abbey was dissolved on 23 September 1538, when the abbot and eight monks signed the document of surrender.

Hulton Abbey has been the subject of extensive archaeological excavations over recent years. The site had been lost until 1884 when land drainage excavations revealed sections of the cloistral buildings. A local architect and antiquarian continued the excavation, recording the ground plan of the precinct and nine stone coffin lids. To date, approximately eighty burials have been excavated, including the graves of abbots and those of members of the Audley family. Most notable among these is the possible burial of Sir William Audley. In 1282 Audley had joined Edward I's army in North Wales. He was among a small group of soldiers ambushed and massacred on Anglesey, and reputedly his body was severely mutilated. A burial at Hulton Abbey contained bones with damage consistent with such a violent death, and it is possible that Sir William's body was returned to Staffordshire for burial.

The excavations have revealed much information about the physical appearance of the abbey. The evidence suggests origins in the early 13th century in the Early English style of architecture. During the 14th and 15th centuries the abbey enjoyed periods of expansion and development, most notably after a bequest by Lady Elizabeth Audley, the last of her line, who died in 1400.

An Augustinian priory was founded at Trentham in about 1150. Trentham Priory was a small foundation and less wealthy than Hulton Abbey. Common grazing rights existed between the two houses and both derived much of their income from the sale of wool. The priory surrendered in 1536 when there were only seven canons, and in 1540 James Leveson acquired the estate. Leveson appears to have been a property speculator capitalising on the Dissolution. His family had amassed considerable wealth as wool merchants, and Leveson had already bought Lilleshall Abbey and Hulton Abbey, although the latter was quickly re-sold. Before settling at Trentham in 1630, the Leveson family made occasional use of their residence. A large house was built in the mid-17th century and was featured in Plot's *Natural History of Staffordshire*.

A period of development and redevelopment followed, culminating with the house of 1833-42 by Sir Charles Barry which Pevsner described as being 'in its own way architecturally as important as the Houses of Parliament'. Unfortunately, it no longer stands, its demolition much mourned by architectural historians. The surviving elements, that is the lake (originally proposed by Capability Brown) and the parterre, both suggest a house of palatial dimensions. Indeed, Trentham was the model for many houses which followed, including Osborne House, the royal residence on the Isle of Wight. Since the demolition in 1911, the gardens have served as a major leisure attraction, with the addition of a ballroom in 1931 and an Art Deco-style swimming pool in 1935. The pool was closed in 1976 and demolished 10 years later.

Churches and chapels are an important feature of the Potteries environment. Arguably one of the most significant churches in the area is the Church of the Holy Trinity on Hartshill Road built in 1842 to designs by George Gilbert Scott. Scott readily acknowledged the influence on his work of Pugin, in a movement rejecting the Gothic as perceived by the Church Commissioners, in favour of a purer and more accurate interpretation of the style. Scott was responsible for much work in the county and was reputedly the architect of the Church of the Resurrection in Longton. Pevsner places some doubt over this.

The cost of the construction of Holy Trinity was borne by the Minton family, or more precisely Herbert Minton, who also paid for the adjoining school and parsonage. These were also designed by Scott. Patronage of church-building by wealthy families and individuals was not uncommon, and apart from the Church Commissioners and church-building societies, it was often the only means by which such projects could be funded. The Duke of Sutherland of Trentham Hall funded the building of the Church of the Holy Evangelists in Normacot in 1847. The Church of St Peter ad Vincula in Stoke cost over £14,000 between 1826 and 1830. The money was raised from a variety of sources including £500 from Josiah Spode and £500 from subscriptions by the people of Stoke-on-Trent.

Nonconformity of religion in a broad sense of the word was particularly active in the Potteries. In an attempt to create their own architectural identity, the Methodist New Connexion rebuilt the Bethesda Chapel in Hanley in an Italianate style between 1819 and

1820. The chapel was given a new façade between 1859 and 1860, whereafter Methodist architecture drew more inspiration from northern Europe. As a movement Methodism had considerable strength in North Staffordshire. John Wesley was a frequent visitor to the Potteries between 1760 and 1790. Following his visit in 1760 one Abraham Lindop opened his own cottage to fellow converts, and in 1766 the first Methodist chapel was built. As Methodism grew in popularity a chapel was built in Swan Bank to seat 1,290 people, and the Charles Street Chapel in Hanley seated 770. By 1851 there were 17 Wesleyan chapels in the area with congregations numbering between 550 and 800. By 1797 there were five meetings of the Methodist New Connexion in the Potteries. The movement almost totally ousted the Wesleyans in Hanley. The Bethesda Chapel seated 2,500, and the congregation included many of the town's most prominent people. At about the same time, Primitive Methodism was born.

The leading figures in this movement were Hugh Bourne, born in Stoke in 1772, and William Clowes, born at Ball Bank in 1780. Bourne became a Methodist in 1799 and observed that the workers were destitute of religion and wished to preach the word of God to 'good or bad, rough or smooth'. He formed a friendship with Clowes who had himself become a Methodist in 1805, following a large open-air prayer meeting in 1807 at Mow Cop on the Staffordshire and Cheshire border. These meetings were emotional events and the authorities, including those in the local Methodist circuit, feared their potential radicalism and subversion. Bourne was expelled from the Burslem circuit in 1808 after denying a ban imposed on these meetings and set up a separate society in 1810, the same year in which Clowes was expelled from the Tunstall circuit. By 1812 their movement which was always strongly identified with working-class evangelism, was known as Primitive Methodism.

Bourne and Clowes are typical of the determination of people from Stoke-on-Trent and its immediate surroundings. A strong workforce drawn from the staple industries of ceramics, coal-mining and steel has produced a number of political and trade union activists, while a wealthy, comfortable middle class has produced literary giants, scientists and sports personalities.

Sarah Bennett came to the Potteries in 1893 and quickly established herself as a trade union activist. She was elected to the Burslem school board, and as an active suffragette she campaigned against the Liberal candidate for North West Staffordshire in 1907 with Christabel Pankhurst. Bennett was one of a line of working-class militants which stretches back beyond the Chartist Movement. Chartism in Stoke-on-Trent was as much about the poor wages and living conditions of the miners and pottery workers, as it was about political reform. After the riots of 1842, local leaders of the Movement endured various terms of imprisonment. However, in time some actually assumed public office. Joseph Capper had spent time in gaol but later served on the local board of health. William Ellis was convicted on largely fabricated evidence and was sentenced to 21 years' transportation to Van Dieman's Land. Jeremiah Yates had run a local coffee-house and distributed radical political pamphlets. He provided accommodation for the itinerant Chartist leader Thomas Cooper when he visited the Potteries. Yates too served time in Stafford gaol, and in later life served as a highway surveyor.

Perhaps the Potteries' most significant scientist was Sir Oliver Lodge, born in Penkhull in 1851. Lodge received a degree from University College, London in 1877 and in 1881 became Professor of Physics and Mathematics at University College, Liverpool. In 1900 he became the first Principal of the University of Birmingham. He was much more than an academic, however. In 1894 he became the first man to transmit a message by radio telegraphy. He also invented the spark plug for the internal combustion engine. His family ran the highly successful Lodge Plug Company. Lodge was an advocate of student representation on the governing bodies of universities, and of women's emancipation. He was also interested in psychic research, conducting many experiments and demonstrations in an attempt to prove the existence of the spirit.

Few will fail to connect the Second World War with one of its most potent symbols—the Spitfire. The success of this aircraft is undisputed and can be credited to the skill and foresight of its designer, Reginald Mitchell, who was born at Butt Lane, Stoke-on-Trent, in 1895. Mitchell died at a tragically early age, before his most famous design flew into action, and of course the marque was to undergo numerous alterations during its service. However, Mitchell's success was not limited to the Spitfire. While working for Supermarine he was instrumental in Britain's Schneider International Seaplane Trophy victories, and he designed many flying boats during the 1920s and 1930s. Throughout the 1920s his designs repeatedly broke the air speed record.

Arguably the most famous person from Stoke-on-Trent is Arnold Bennett. Born in Hanley in 1867, Bennett with his family endured poverty while his father studied to become a solicitor. After he gained his qualifications in 1879, the family moved to Burslem, and Arnold was encouraged to take up law. He failed his examinations, however, and in 1889 moved to London where he took up freelance writing. After 1900 he concentrated on plays and novels with some freelance journalism, and became increasingly wealthy. His work reflected life in the Potteries although he rarely returned to the city. He wrote, amongst many other volumes, *Anna of the Five Towns*, which has erroneously led to the idea of the five instead of six pottery towns, and the famous *Clayhanger* trilogy. These have been serialised for television and are accurate reflections of relationships in an industrialised city. Bennett died in 1931 and his ashes were buried in the family grave in Burslem.

A history of Stoke-on-Trent, no matter how brief, would not be complete without some consideration of the industry for which the city is most famous. An identifiable trend towards the pottery industry existed from at least the medieval period, but the potters operated on a small scale, producing wares for the local market. Some potters sought to be little more than self-sufficient, although a concept of commerciality always existed. The backbone of the emerging industry was the production of items required for everyday use. This has continued through to the modern period and tableware from Stoke-on-Trent today enjoys an enviable, international reputation.

One reason why the Potteries emerged as a centre for ceramics was the proximity of certain essential resources, particularly of large coalfields. Local clays were not abundant enough to sustain the industry without importing from elsewhere in the country, particularly from Cornwall. However, the local coal measures were rich, a factor which influenced the 18th-century entrepreneurs. The Trent and Mersey Canal, which began construction in 1766, connected the city with the major ports. As a result large quantities of materials could now be moved into Stoke, and the finished products could be shipped to Liverpool and thence the world. The canal also allowed large unwieldy cargoes of flint and ground animal bone to be easily transported between suppliers and potbanks within the city. It is surprising therefore that not all potbanks were located close to the canal system. Many were established some distance away, but were closer to the coalfields to reduce the burden and costs of moving fuel.

Potbanks are a group of buildings and kilns around a central yard. The bottle ovens were the dominant structures, originally free standing but often in later years partially enclosed by other buildings. The yards often appeared cluttered, with little rationale behind the planning, but the façade of the buildings, that which overlooked the street, was often a well-designed and significant piece of architecture. Designs were frequently taken from classical architecture, although Enoch Wood's works at Burslem with its castellation and Gothic appearance was a striking exception.

It was Wedgwood's Etruria Works which most potbanks attempted to emulate, although the concept behind Etruria was more far-reaching. Wedgwood was attempting to create the ideal work environment. Etruria opened in 1769 and to an extent the design reflected Wedgwood's own ideas, although he worked with Joseph Pickford of Derby. The same architect also designed the adjacent Etruria Hall in which Wedgwood and his family lived.

Etruria took its name from that part of Italy from which came a style of classical pottery Wedgwood imitated. No doubt the refinement and qualities Wedgwood saw in this pottery he intended to be reflected in his factory and model village. However, in practice the workers' housing at Etruria reflected styles already used elsewhere in the Potteries, and a school and chapel were only introduced under a separate scheme. The houses consisted of four rooms, the plain front door opening into the living room. Pumps and water wells were provided for groups of three houses. Workers were also able to bake their own bread in communal bakeries of which there were several. Clearly Wedgwood's main motivation was to house his workforce in close proximity to the factory, Etruria at that time being some distance from the other towns.

What was different within Etruria was the overall layout. Etruria Hall, situated on a hill, overlooked an artificially created landscape in which ornamental grounds fell away from the house to two lakes. Close by ran the Trent and Mersey Canal along which stood Wedgwood's factory. There is no evidence to support the theory that Capability Brown was involved in the design of this landscape. Wedgwood probably put into effect his own designs, as he had with the house; Etruria Hall was constructed to a square plan and built of brick with stone dressings. The central three bays were pedimented and flanked by one bay each side. Extensions have been made to the Hall during its history, but no original fittings or fixtures other than a fire grate appear to have survived.

In 1844 the house and estate were put up for sale by the Wedgwood family. At that time the house was said to have 34 rooms. The reserve price was not met and parts of the estate were sold off in a random manner. Etruria Hall was eventually sold in 1851 to the Duchy of Lancaster who in 1860 let it to the 4th Earl of Granville. The estate gradually became heavily industrialised. Granville was a colliery owner who sank shafts in the area, expanding his business with the arrival of the railways in 1848. The Granville family also operated ironworks, and in 1850 new furnaces were built along the Trent and Mersey Canal at Etruria. This development of mining and iron production continued and the Shelton Iron Steel and Oil Company was formed in 1888.

By the turn of the 20th century what had been a model factory and living environment had become a village surrounded by the debris of heavy industry. Wedgwood's factory deteriorated, resulting in production being transferred to Barlaston outside the city in 1940. The original Wedgwood factory was demolished in 1960 with the exception of the Round-house. From the 1970s the steel industry has continued to contract, leaving the environment devastated. The 1986 National Garden Festival was held on part of the site and resulted in an influx of development funds, and the construction of trade and industrial estates and extensive leisure facilities. The site of Wedgwood's factory is now that of the local *Evening Sentinel* newspaper's production plant, of which the Roundhouse is a fleeting feature to passing motorists using the adjacent dual carriageway. Etruria Hall has been refurbished as a hotel.

Communication networks have played an important rôle in the development of the Staffordshire Potteries. Canals were significant in the opening up of this landlocked area of the Midlands to the main ports, particularly Liverpool. The county of Staffordshire before the 18th century was without any navigable rivers, although the Stow, Trent, Severn and Weaver rivers were within close distance and these all enjoyed some degree of improvement to allow passage of traffic. The idea of using canals in the emergent Potteries gained early acceptance; the economy of canal building compared to turnpike roads, and the improved safety of fragile cargoes were cited as good reasons. By the 1760s the successful precedent of the Duke of Bridgwater's canal between Manchester and Runcorn had become an added incentive and the Duke's engineer, James Brindley, was employed to survey and construct what was to become Staffordshire's first canal, the Trent and Mersey. Josiah Wedgwood was committed to the project, seeing the benefits a canal would bring to his business, situated as it was along the line of the proposed cutting. It was Wedgwood who was to cut the first sod on 26 July 1766. Other canals soon followed of which the Caldon, Newcastle, Uttoxeter and Staffordshire and Worcestershire are examples. The Birmingham canal was begun in 1768 with the aim of carrying coal, and upon its completion in 1772 quickly surpassed road transport for such a bulky commodity.

Coal mining in North Staffordshire has been a staple industry in its own right, and its importance increased dramatically with the use of fossil fuels in the pottery industry. The coalfield lies in four main areas: Cheadle, Goldsitch Moss, the Potteries and Shaffalong. The Potteries field is pre-eminent. Coal extraction may have been carried out in the North Staffordshire area since the 2nd century A.D., but until the mid-16th century the industry served very localised needs and expanded very slowly. Overall, the industry expanded rapidly after c.1750, and continued to be a major employer until the second half of the 20th century. Economic and political policies resulted in the closure of many pits during the 1980s, and the year-long miners' strike of 1984-85 was bitterly fought in North Staffordshire. Whole communities were mobilised in a fight to save jobs, and support groups such as the Miners' Wives Action Groups did much to raise public awareness of the issues. In the City Museum and Art Gallery in Hanley stands a sculpture dedicated to all those who took part in the strike.

Since 1945 much has been done to improve the quality of life in the Potteries. Various measures to reduce air pollution have been successful, but this has to be seen in the context of the decline in the use of the traditional bottle ovens. Many of these structures have now been demolished and, of those which survive, none are now fired. The Gladstone Pottery Museum in Longton preserves one of the last groupings of such kilns in the city and the museum interprets the working and social history of a potbank. The success in cleaning up the air and improving the whole environment can be seen in the annual health reports. In 1910 the biggest cause of death in Stoke-on-Trent was disease related to the respiratory system. Tuberculosis and other infectious diseases accounted for 23 per cent of all deaths in the area, with heart diseases accounting for 7.4 per cent and cancer for 4 per cent. By 1992 circulatory diseases accounted for 47.8 per cent of all deaths, respiratory causes of death having been reduced to third place behind cancers.

The postwar years have seen a shift in the economic base of the Potteries. The ceramics industry is a cornerstone of an increasing heritage and culture enterprise. It is strongly represented in the City Museum and Art Gallery, as well as in museums operated by the larger manufacturers such as Wedgwood and Spode. Service industries to the potbanks such as bone and flint crushing are interpreted at the Etruria Industrial Museum, formerly the works of Jesse Shirley and Sons whose business still operates adjacent to the site. This site is also located at the junction of the Caldon and the Trent and Mersey Canals, illustrating the importance of the canal network to the industry. Other leisure facilities have been developed, such as a cinema complex and large swimming baths on the site of the National Garden Festival. Concerns have been raised about such sites draining life away from the city's centre, concerns which have been or will be addressed.

Hanley has emerged as the commercial centre of the city. The large Potteries Shopping Centre draws shoppers from a wide regional catchment area. Stoke itself remains the administrative core of the Six Towns. The recently expanded Civic Centre will be the focus of a new authority with unitary status.

1 An impression of Hulton Abbey cloistral precinct soon after its foundation in 1223. The abbey included service buildings such as a smithy, an infirmary and a bakehouse, all of which were grouped around an outer court.

2 Cut away illustration of the Abbey church. Altars were located in chapels in both transepts in addition to the high altar. A 19th-century farmhouse had been built over much of the north transept. The church had both north and south aisles with lancet windows at east and west ends.

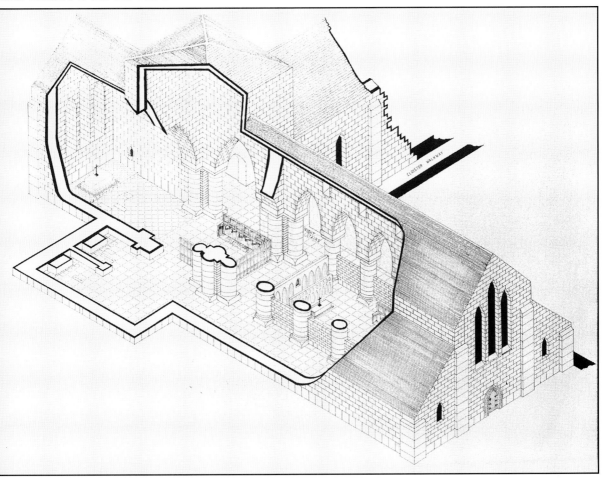

3 The night stairs led from the first-floor dormitor of the east range into the Abbey church, opposite th two chapels in the south transept.

4 Archaeological evidence suggests this form for the chapter house of Hulton Abbey during the 13th century.

5 Cruck-framed house, Milton. Ironically many of the early buildings in the city were recorded only at the time of their demolition. The cruck frame is clearly visible in this house in Easters Road in 1960.

6 Parker Street, Burslem. A terrace typical of many industrial towns and cities. A rough road surface is flanked by cobbled drainage and in the distance are several bottle kilns, pollution from which would have permeated these houses.

7 Milner Street, Hanley. The area around the Bell Works and the Bethesda Chapel was once heavily populated, with streets such as this running off Bethesda Street. Today the area is largely covered by the City Museum, the reference library, a police station, magistrates' courts and a multi-storey car park.

8 Ricardo Street, Dresden. Dresden lies near Longton, and Ricardo Street boasts varying styles of architecture

9 Late 19th-century housing, Victoria Place in Fenton, photographed in 1973. To this day there remains much 19th- and early 20th-century housing, although large areas have been cleared for modern housing or commercial developments.

10 The various industries of the area generated wealth for the factory owners who were able to afford substantial houses. A luxury such as ice for refrigeration was stored in ice houses like this one at Hartshill.

11 Master potters commanded much higher wages and lived in comparative luxury. This house in Manor Street, Fenton was possibly a master potter's residence, and served as offices when this photograph was taken in 1975.

12 Century Street, Hanley c.1900. The dominance of the bottle ovens is clearly visible and the problems of pollution cannot be escaped.

3 Workers' houses are dwarfed by the bottle ovens in this view across Longton. Pottery workers often had little choice
ut to live in close proximity to their workplace. As a result their children grew up knowing little of life beyond this
nvironment, and often followed their parents into the potbanks.

Jug Bank

14 Jug Bank, Cobridge, 1929. Jug Bank lay off Sneyd Street South. This view was taken near to a blacksmith's shop and the *Jug* public house.

15 Chase Lodge, Tittensor, January 1913. Views such as, to the south of the city, show an immediate contrast with the environment of Stoke.

6 Middle John Street was part of an area of housing off High Street, Longton. The area was demolished in 1935 after
a strong case for clearance had been put forward by the corporation's housing department. In this photograph a wall of
saggars has been built between numbers 15 and 17.

17 The *Sea Lion* inn stood on the corner of John Street and Upper John Street. It was one of two public houses along the street, and was the scene of many Saturday night fights.

18 Lower John Street is recalled as being the worst place in the area to live. The street was blocked at one end by a factory wall.

19 Meirhay Road towards the Shraft Ruk or wasteland. The road was considered to be the more respectable part of the area and was not demolished.

20 Dated 1757, this house was built by Thomas and John Wedgwood. It was on the steps of this house that Josiah Heapy was shot dead during the Chartist Riots of 1842. He was allegedly throwing stones at the militia, and a verdict of justifiable homicide was returned.

21 Until its demolition in 1939, Longton Hall was undoubtedly the most important building in the town. An earlier manor house existed on the site prior to extensive alterations in the late 1770s by John Edensor Heathcote. The Heathcote family had extensive land holdings in the area and continued to live at the Hall until *c*.1840, after which it was leased.

22 Trentham Hall was considered by Pevsner to be architecturally as important as the Houses of Parliament. Designed by Sir Charles Barry and built between 1833-42, it was the seat of the Duke and Duchess of Sutherland. It was demolished early this century and the extensive grounds now form a leisure park.

3 A photograph across the formal gardens taken in the late 19th century, showing the magnificence of Barry's design. Italianate in influence, Trentham Hall was undoubtedly the most impressive building in the region.

24 Work in progress on the demolition of Trentham Hall, 1911. Building materials were salvaged and sold.

25 Ice-skating was popular in Trentham Park even before the demolition of the Hall. This photograph was taken in February 1912.

26 Stoke City met Arsenal in the sixth round of the 1928 F.A. Cup. Unfortunately Stoke lost 4-1. Sir Stanley Matthews, one of the most respected and well-known players of all time, played for Stoke and still maintains close contact with the town and the sport.

27 Port Vale in action at the recreation ground in Hanley, where the team played between 1913 and 1950. The club's ground is now at Vale Park in Burslem.

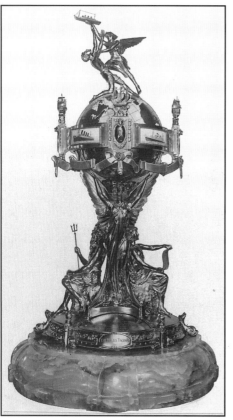

28 The Hales Trophy, otherwise known as the Blue Riband, has been contested by the United States and Britain for the fastest transatlantic crossing. It was designed by the Hanley-based jewellers, Pidduck and Sons, but has remained in America.

29 Hot-air balloon, Hanley Park. The parks in the city were obvious locations for the popular fairs and festivals which took place around the time of the Potters' Holidays. Many workers did not travel away for their holidays, but when they did it was often to the North Wales coast, Blackpool or Southport.

30 Hanley Park fountain. As well as providing town halls to foster civic pride, each of the towns invested in a park for the enjoyment of all. The exception was Stoke, the councillors arguing that the close proximity of Hanley Park would suffice.

31 Plan of Hanley Park showing the range of facilities to be available to the people of the town. These included tennis courts, a bowling green, a boating lake and a children's playground.

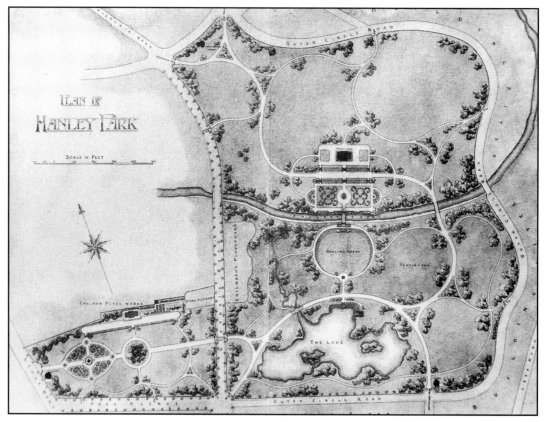

32 View of Burslem Park, c.1902. The park was built
over a former colliery, the sealed pithead being covered
by the ornamental lake.

33 A view showing the boating lake in Queen's Park,
Longton. Boating was popular in the Potteries. The
photograph also illustrates the attention to detail in the
layout and upkeep of the park.

34 This topiary house stood in Longton Park throughout the 1930s and was one of the more unusual features.

35 Longton War Memorial. This is the most impressive memorial in the city and stands outside Longton Park.

66 Willow Pattern Gardens, Biddulph Grange, *c*.1860. The gardens at Biddulph were begun in 1845. They were conceived by James Bateman and are laid out in a series of themes based on cultures of the world such as the Egyptian Court and the Chinese Pagoda. The gardens were acquired by the National Trust in 1988.

67 Biddulph Old Hall. A 17th-century house attached to an Elizabethan mansion. Built by the Biddulph family in the 1580s, the house was put under siege by Parliamentarian forces during the Civil War and was eventually sacked.

38 Architectural detail, Biddulph Old Hall, 195? The remains of the Old Hall are significant bu may only be seen by arrangement.

39 Biddulph Grange was built in 1876 to a desig by Thomas Bower. It has had a chequered histor and actually served as a hospital between 1928 ar c.1990. The gardens are now owned by the Nation Trust.

0 (*right*) Mow Cop, a folly built in 1754 to improve the horizon as seen from Rode Hall. It stands on an outcrop of rock on the Cheshire and Staffordshire border.

1 (*below*) Mow Cop, an impromptu meeting, 1907. Primitive Methodism had been founded at Mow Cop following a large open-air rally. Large evangelical meetings frequently took place on the site despite official condemnation because of their alleged subversion.

2 (*right*) Bethesda Chapel, Hanley. The chequered brickwork is a distinctive feature behind the Italianate façade. The chapel dates from 1819 but the façade from 1859. The scale of the chapel reflects the importance of Methodism in the town.

43 Interior of the Charles Street Chapel. The rich decoration of flowers and vegetables suggests that a harvest festival service was due to take place.

4 View of the north side of St John the Baptist Church, Hanley. Now redundant, it is thought that the building is a rare example of a steel-framed church. Built between 1788 and 1790, a polygonal apse was added in 1872.

45 All Saints Church, Hanley. Standing on Leek Road, All Saints was designed by Gerald Horsley and built between 1910 and 1913. There is a clerestory above the north aisle, but the south is strikingly absent in this photograph.

46 Wolstanton Church. The church is a significant landmark and dates from 1859-60. It is in the Early English and Decorated styles.

47 Well-dressing is an ancient custom preceding the introduction of Christianity. This photograph of Endon well in 1928 shows how the practice had acquired Christian beliefs.

48 The well-dressing at Endon was accompanied by local festivities, including a fair and what would appear to be a 'Queen' for the event. This photograph was taken in the early 1950s.

49 Molly Leigh, whose cottage is illustrated here, endured the reputation of being a witch and many superstitions surround her grave in Burslem.

50 Shelton Old Hall, thought to be the birthplace of the poet Elijah Fenton, 1683-1730. Fenton was acknowledged by Dr. Johnson as 'an excellent versifier and a good poet', but was known also for his life of ease.

51 Edward John Smith, 1850-1912. Smith is renowned for being the captain of the ill-fated *Titanic*. Of humble origins, Smith rose to be a highly accomplished mariner, passing his Master's examinations at an early age and becoming the White Star Line's principal commodore. He captained many of their prestige liners, including the *Titanic*'s sister ship, the *Olympic*.

52 Sir Oliver Lodge, 1857-1940. Lodge's career was one of great achievement. He became the first Principal of Birmingham University in 1900, but his greatest contributions lie in his invention of the spark plug for use in motor engines, and in being the first person to transmit a message by radio telegraphy in 1894.

53 Arnold Bennett, 1867-1931. The novels of Bennett were based around Burslem; some of the buildings he used in the stories still survive. He left the Potteries in 1889 for a career in London and during the 1890s established his reputation as a writer. His ashes are buried in Burslem.

54   Havergal Brian, 1876-1972. Born at 35 Ricardo Street in Dresden, near Longton, Brian developed musical skills at an early age, eventually turning to composition. Largely self-taught, his first success was a setting for Shakespeare's sonnet *Shall I Compare Thee to a Summer's Day*. In 1966 his Gothic Symphony was performed at the Royal Albert Hall with Sir Adrian Boult. He was acquainted with Arnold Bennett, for whom this photograph is signed.

55 Gertie Gitana (Gertrude Astbury), 1888-1957. Gert[ie] Gitana was a popular music-hall artist from Hanley. She w[as] born in Longton, and her family had moved to Hanley by h[er] fourth birthday when she was already considered a prodig[y]. She starred in many stage successes in London. Her sta[ge] career ended in 1948 after a three-year run in *Thanks for t[he] Memory* and an appearance at the Royal Variety Performanc[e].

56 Reginald J. Mitchell, 1895-1937. Mitchell was born at Butt Lane, the son of a headmaster at Longton who went on to become a printer. Mitchell was educated at Hanley High School and the Wedgwood Technical School in Burslem. On gaining employment at the Supermarine Aviation Works in Southampton, he quickly became Chief Designer and Engineer, and masterminded the success of the company in the Schneider International Seaplane Trophy in the 1920s. He designed several military aircraft, chief of which was the Spitfire which became the symbol of British resistance and success during the war.

7 Josiah Wedgwood, 1730-1795. Wedgwood is synonymous with the pottery industry, the development of ceramic technology and the entrepreneurial spirit which led to the creation of the industry in the area. He developed a model factory in Etruria and had a philanthropic attitude towards his workforce. (*Trustees of the Wedgwood Museum, Barlaston, Staffs.*)

58 Jeremiah Yates, 1808-1852. Yates was one of the leading figures in the Chartist Movement in the Potteries. He ran a coffee-house, used as a meeting place in which he provided rooms for Thomas Cooper, the itinerant Chartist speaker. Having served a sentence for his involvement in the movement, Yates went on to serve in public office.

59 In 1930 to celebrate the bicentenary of Wedgwood's birth the city held a pageant in Hanley Park in which scenes from history were re-enacted. The Chartist riots of 1842 featured in the pageant and this still from a movie made of the event depicts Thomas Cooper addressing the crowds.

60 Another still from the 1930 movie in which the crowds clash with the militia in the 1842 riots. In the original riots the crowds were large, with marchers arriving from nearby Macclesfield, Congleton and even Manchester.

61 *Mixed Industry,* 1937 by C.W. Brown (1882-1961). Locally-born artist Brown spent most of his working life in the Staffordshire coalfields. Art was his life-long hobby and one which became more productive after his retirement in 1948. Many of his paintings depict the industry, environment and people of the Potteries.

62 During the miners' strike of 1912, people salvaged what fuel they could from the waste tips. This photograph wa
taken in the Longton area.

63 Miners established small camps and excavations during the 1912 strike, desperately seeking coal.

4 The Jamage Rescue Brigade, January 1918. Collieries in Stoke have suffered their share of disasters, for example Jamage itself in 1911 when six men died. The worst disaster occurred at the Minnie Pit in January 1918 when rescue teams were deployed from all over the region. A total of 115 miners lost their lives in the disaster.

In Loving Memory of the Men and Boys

Who lost their lives by the MINNIE PIT Colliery Explosion (near Stoke) on the morning of Saturday, January 12th, 1918, whereby 160 Souls were launched in eternity.

NOW the day of toil is done,
Now the race of life is run,
Father, grant thy wearied ones
Rest for evermore!

Now the strife of sin is stilled,
Now the foe within is killed,
By Thy gracious Word fulfilled,
Peace for evermore!

Now that darkness melts away
At the breaking of Thy day,
Bid them hail the cheering ray;
Light for evermore!

Now the breath of life has flown,
Now the grave must claim its own,
Lord of Life! be their's Thy crown,
Life for evermore!

names of some of the
160 VICTIMS:

L Rowley, Heathcotes road, Halmer End
J Ampson, Scot Hay road, Alsagers Bank
T Cope, High street, Halmer End
J Lee, Scot Hay road, Alsagers Bank
G Browning, Chapel street, Audley
V Rowley, Chesterton road, Audley
S Heeley, Heathcote road, Halmer End
E Lee, High street, Halmer End.
E Holland, Shraley Brook
T West, Wynnbrook, Audley
G Rowley, Heathcote road, Audley
H Warsham, High street, Alsagers Bank
R Pointon, High street, Alsagers Bank
E Holland, Chapel lane, Shraley Brook
J Richardson, Station road, Miles Green
T Timmis, King street, Wearton road, Audley
F Rhodes, Mellard street, Audley
P Benson, 29 Heathcote road, Miles Green
J Jones, 65 High street, Alsagers Bank
-- Doorbar (one of the rescue party, died in the mine)
G Plant, Wearton road, Audley
G Brown, Hall Hall street, Audley

R. I. P.

65 Commemorative tissue for the Minnie P[it] disaster of 12 January 1918. Some of th[e] casualties are listed on the tissue.

66 During the 1984-5 miners' strike, the wiv[es] of striking miners formed active support group[s] raising money and keeping the issues of th[e] strike in the public eye. Their support an[d] contribution has been recognised at the highe[st] levels of the National Union of Mineworker[s]

7 The North Staffordshire Miners' Wives Action Group commissioned a sculpture to commemorate the strike. It was sculpted from local coal by Frank Casey and stands in the City Museum and Art Gallery.

8 Taylor's Chain Works, Smallthorne. Chain-making was a relatively small industry in the area and few records survive. However, independent and small-scale factories such as this were very important regarding the supply of the larger firms.

69 Flint-milling was an important subsidiary industry to that of pottery manufacture. Raw materials were brought down from the Staffordshire moorlands and the Pennines on the Caldon Canal to mills such as that of George Edwards and Sons at Bucknall.

70 The Etruscan Bone and Flint Mill operated by the company of Jessie Shirley supplied bone and flint to the main pottery businesses. Flint was heated and broken in the kiln, while bone supplied from abattoirs was ground to fine powder in pans in the mill. Power was supplied to the pans by a steam engine. Shirley's continue to expand their business to the rear of the mill moving into advanced ceramics. The original buildings are now part of an industrial museum.

71 A shraft and marl pit in Longton, *c*.1900. Marl pits were common in the city and were often filled in with waste or shraft. Broken and substandard pottery was salvaged for use.

72   Hanford Brick and Tile Company, *c.*1920. An aerial view of a factory covering the site of a Roman kiln of *c.*A.D.60
It is now the location of Michelin Tyres, a major employer in the city.

73 The site of the Bell Works is now occupied by the City Museum and Art Gallery. The houses which surround the potbank have also disappeared. The works reputedly served as an arsenal of ammunition during the war.

74 The façade of the Bell Works during the postwar years. No longer solely a pottery works, footwear, furnishings and tailoring service are all advertised.

75 Walter Sylvester Ltd. at the junction of Williamson Street and Scotia Road, Tunstall in 1950. The bridge carried the Staffordshire loopline railway.

76 The factory of Enoch Wood in Burslem. The design is in marked contrast to the designs of many other potbanks in the area.

77 The bottle kilns of Samuel Radford's China Works in Fenton stand quiet in this photograph of 1950.

78 A view along Crane Street, Cobridge, towards Myott's Works in about 1930. Crates for the packaging of pottery await removal from outside the works.

79 A typical example of a potbank layout with a yard containing packaging barrels in front of a series of kilns.

0 Saggar maker's workshop, Longton. Saggars were essential in
e firing of pottery. Made of baked clay, saggars contained the pottery
hilst in the kiln. They would be stacked on top of each other,
inimising breakages.

1 Inside the kiln the saggars containing the pottery were stacked
rior to firing. Workers often carried the saggars on their heads.
tacking the saggars was called 'setting in'.

82 A fireman fuels the fire within a kiln. A stack of saggars stands behind him.

83 Women were employed extensively in the pottery industry in both manual and administrative rôles. The location of this photograph is not known, but it does show the volume of wares prior to packing. Women were often employed to assess for quality.

84 Packing was important for the industry. To prevent breakages the pottery was packed in straw and placed in crates. Potbanks employed skilled packers and cratemakers.

85 Wedgwood's factory at Etruria. This view taken in the early 20th century shows the extent to which Wedgwood's rural Etruria had disappeared under heavy industry. The Roundhouse in the foreground is all that remains.

86 The Roundhouse at Etruria after the removal of Wedgwood's works to Barlaston. The purpose of the structure is unknown, but it was once one of a pair.

87 A bleak industrial landscape from Bedford Street towards the Shelton Iron and Steelworks in October 1960. This view demonstrates again the discrepancy between the ideal working and living environment which Wedgwood had envisaged for this site, and the actual progress of industrialisation during the following centuries.

88 A graphic example of the effects of marl extraction and waste dumping. Many such sites have been reclaimed and built upon, or turned into open spaces.

89 Allotments have been maintained by the city despite pressure for land use. Today's younger generation of gardeners have taken on allotments and participate in a thriving form of popular culture.

0 Fêtes and carnivals attract people in fancy dress. This group of people revived 19th-century costume for a Carnival at Cheadle in July 1933.

In 1952 a parade was held in Bradeley to raise funds for the local hospital. One of the draught horses was dressed ready for the procession. Even in the early years the National Health Service relied on public generosity for much-needed funding.

INDEPENDENT ORDER OF
GOOD TEMPLARS

"HOPE OF ALSAGER" LODGE
NO. 1333.

THE FIRST GRAND ANNUAL

DEMONSTRATION
AND
FESTIVAL!

In connection with the above Good Templar Hall Building Fund, will be held

IN A FIELD AT ALSAGER,
On STOKE WAKES THURSDAY
AUGUST 7TH 1873.

THE PROCESSION will start from the Lodge Room, Primitive Methodist School, at 2-30 p.m. and Patrol the Village to the Field.

The Tunstall St. Mary's Lodge Brass Band,
(20 Instruments) will head the Procession and Play at Intervals.

The Committee have great pleasure in announcing that they have secured the services of

R. P. J. SIMPSON, Esq. District Deputy, of West Cheshire; DAVID ROBERTS Esq., of Chester; W. BEARDMORE, Esq. of Newcastle; and other Leading Gentlemen of the Order to deliver ADDRESSES at the Public Meeting.

Chair to be taken at Seven o'clock.

BALLOONS WILL ASCEND AT INTERVALS.

VARIOUS SPORTS AND OTHER
AMUSEMENTS!
WILL BE INTRODUCED.
The whole to conclude with a Display of Fireworks.

Refreshments of all Descriptions provided on the Field.   Admission 6d. each.

☞ N.B.—All Lodges are particularly invited to attend, and appear in regalia to join in Procession.

A SPECIAL TRAIN will leave STOKE at 1-40; ETRURIA, 1-46; Burslem or LONGPORT 1-53; Tunstall or CHATTERLEY 1-58; HARECASTLE, 2-5, P.M. Returning from Alsager at 10-0 p.m.

FARES THERE & BACK Stoke and Etruria. First Class. **2**s.   Third Class. **1**s.
Longport or Burslem ditto. **1**s.**6**d.   ditto. **9**d.
Chatterley & Harecastle ORDINARY FARES.   Children under **12** Half Price.

I. B. Shaw, Printer, Stationer, and Bookbinder, High Street, Tunstall.

92 Stoke Wakes' Week affected the surrounding communities. In 1873 the neighbouring village of Alsager held a processsion featuring the brass band of Tunstall St Mary's Lodge. Various sports and other amusements were promised!

3 Works' outing for employees of H.R. Johnson, tile manufacturers, *c.*1910. Manufacturers appear to have maintained morale and loyalty through such outings.

94 Borough of Burslem Horticultural Show and Fête Committee of 1907. Horticulture has always been popular in the Potteries. Even today allotments are in great demand for both recreational purposes, and to supplement family diets. The annual show is still a major event in the Victoria Hall in Hanley.

95 Miss Joyce Freeman won the first Miss Stoke-on-Trent Pageant in 1950. This photograph was taken at Port Vale F.C.'s old ground in Hanley.

96 Hanley Town Prize Band in Burslem Park, *c*.1910. The four brothers survived the First World War, but their father was killed in action in 1916.

In 1924 Cross Street School, Stoke won a competition for local choirs held in the Victoria Hall, Hanley. This photograph was taken in the school playground.

98 Cross Street School continued their success in 1926, winning a competition held in Hanley Park. On both occasions the choirmaster was Sam Goodall.

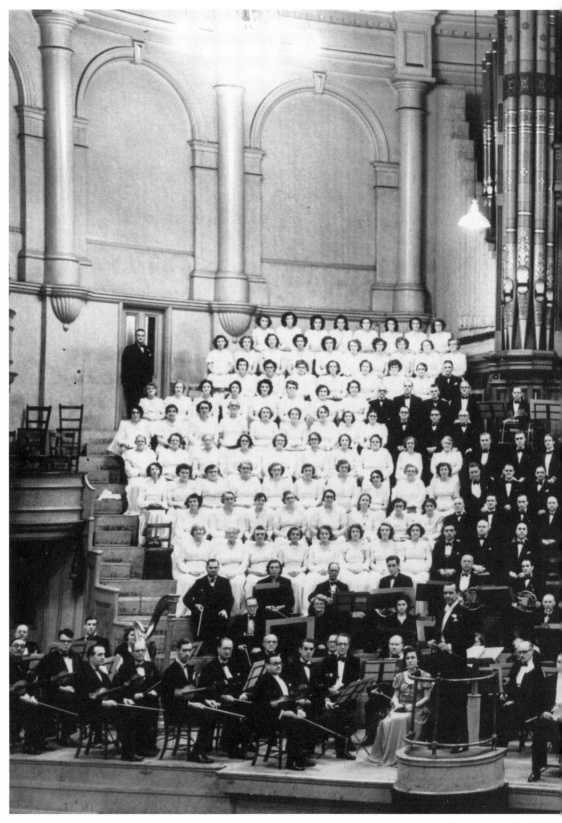

99 The Ceramic City Choir is perhaps the most famous from the Potteries. Formed during the war, the choir first performed at the Victoria Hall in 1942, conducted by Malcolm Sargent. Sargent was the regular conductor and enjoyed an international reputation. The photograph shows the choir ready to perform *Hiawatha* in 1949.

100 The Grand Theatre, Hanley, was a popular music-hall and variety theatre which in later life converted to a cinema. The building was destroyed by fire in the early 1930s.

101 The Theatre Royal, Hanley, has a mixed history but has attracted many stars. Only recently it operated as a bingo hall until a consortium bought the building and reopened the theatre. The building stands on the site of a former Chartist meeting house and a pit-head.

102 In June 1949 the Theatre Royal was devastated by fire. A theatre has stood on the site since the 1840s, the present building dating from 1951.

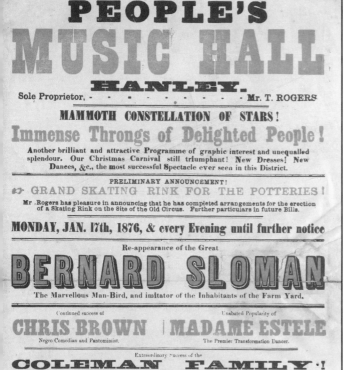

103 Poster advertising attractions at the People's Music Hall, Hanley, from 17 January 1876 onwards and promising 'Immense Throngs of Delighted People'.

104 The Alhambra cinema, Longton, was demolished in 1994 in a major road development, although the façade of the building has been preserved.

RITZ CINEMA, TUNSTALL

(By kind permission of the Directors)

SUNDAY, MARCH 25th, 1945, AT 6-30

HOWARD W. RUDD presents

'Personalities on War Work'

A Grand Variety Concert by the Staff of a Midlands War Factory.

AL TURNER (Tenor)   FLORENCE SMITHSON (Soprano)
WILSON MOULD (Tenor)   HORACE FROST (Mimic)
            HAROLD BARLOW (Solo Pianoforte)
RAY WINNET (Vicar of Mirth)   FRED LINES (Ace Acordionist)

The Personality Quintet

Mixed Voice Choir of 30 Performers

And HOWARD W. RUDD

Comedian, Character Actor and Compere

★ AN ENTERTAINMENT FOR ALL AGES ★
Clean - Neat - Amusing - Non-Stop

Admission 3/6 (Numbered and Reserved) 2/6 1/6 1/-

The whole Cast is giving its Services Free

Entire Proceeds for the Soldiers', Sailors' and Airmen's Families Association.

105 Poster advertising the 'Personalities at War Work' concert at the Ritz Cinema, Tunstall, on 25 March 1945. The concert raised money for the Soldiers', Sailors' and Airmen's Families Association.

106 The Odeon, Hanley, 1958. Built on the site of the Grand Theatre in the 1930s, and typical of Odeon cinemas throughout the country. Recently out of town multi-screen complexes, offering a varied programme and restaurants, cafés and other amusements, have forced the closure of small cinemas. The Odeon closed in 1975, recently reopening as a wine bar.

07 The Odeon, Hanley. Movies have always been popular. It can be as difficult to see a major new film today as it was to see Hitchcock's *Psycho*.

108 Hanley Museum and Art Gallery, Pall Mall, 1930. The museum had been extended in 1927 to accommodate an art gallery, but this building was demolished in 1956.

109 The demolition of the Museum and Art Gallery. Hanley town hall stands in the distance.

110 City Museum and Art Gallery, 1956. The Museum was relocated from Pall Mall to Bethesda Street, the new building costing £46,000. It has now largely disappeared within the development of the current building, completed in the 1980s.

111 The Wedgwood Institute was opened in 1869 to a design by R. Edgar and J.L. Lapling. It served as an educational and cultural centre—the terracotta and brick façade represents the months and the signs of the zodiac. The foundation stone was laid by William Gladstone.

112 The Sutherland Institute, Longton. An imposing building serving as a library, built between 1897 and 1899. The terracotta relief frieze illustrates the pottery industry and dates from 1908-1909.

113 Brick House Street, Burslem. A photograph taken from Queen Street and looking towards the Market Place. It was also known as Cock Alley; poultry were slaughtered there before being sold at market.

114 The Co-operative movement was active in the Potteries. The first shop of the Burslem Industrial Co-operative Society was in Newcastle Street.

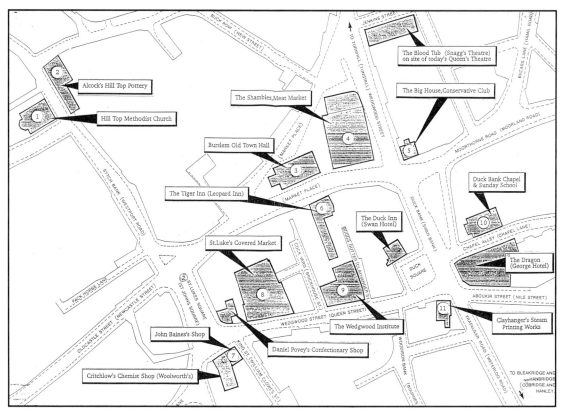

115 A map of Burslem showing the location of some of the more significant buildings which appeared in the works of Arnold Bennett. The name in brackets is the true name of each site.

116 The classical design of the town hall and market hall in Burslem during the early 19th century indicates the wea
and aspirations of the town claiming to be the mother town of the Potteries.

17 A Burslem to Smallthorne tram outside the Big House in Burslem. The town hall in the background is surrounded y scaffolding.

18 View along Leek Road in Smallthorne at the turn of the century. Smallthorne was a sizeable township with 6,000 habitants in 1896. It had its own railway station and several chapels in addition to St Saviour's Church. The children this photograph contrast sharply with the fashionable woman at the right of the picture, whose hemline falls above her nkles.

119 Cobridge Fire Brigade, *c*.1885. Before Federation the towns operated their own essential services such as police and fire brigades. The fire engine was often housed in the town hall.

0 Like other pottery towns, Burslem operated its own police force, photographed here in 1895. In common with the fire
gade it had its headquarters at the town hall; only later did it move to its own station.

121 Shelton Church dominates the skyline of Etruria and Shelton in this photograph taken in 1961. The picture was taken from near the junction of the Caldon and the Trent and Mersey Canals. The Caldon Canal was mainly used for transporting heavy loads of stone to the Potteries.

122 A British Waterways vessel with cargo in Shelton, 1961.

123 Drawbridge, Newcastle Canal, November 1913. The tranquility of the scene between Trent Vale and Newcastle belies the industry of the area and the original function of the canal.

124 Mabel Cartwright outside a shop in Trent Vale in the early 1920s. The shop window displays a mixture of clothes and fashion accessories, with advertisements for Oxo and Cadbury's.

125 Public transport in the Potteries has largely been in the hands of the Potteries Midlands Transport Company. This photograph shows a driver in the company uniform of the 1930s.

126 Tram car no. 22, built in Preston in 1898. It originally served as a trailer car, but was later fitted with its own motor. The poster advertises a performance at the Theatre Royal, Hanley.

27 An advertisement for the business of Tom Smith of Hanley which built and repaired vehicles. It is interesting that farm vehicles were given such importance in a predominantly industrialised area.

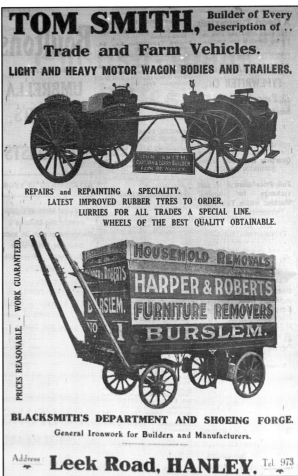

28 A traction engine rolls through the village of Bignall End in this pre-1914 view. The scene is chiefly rural although several mines existed in the area.

129 A double-decker bus travelling up Whitfield Road. The tram system eventually gave way to improved roads and the bus companies.

130 View of Meir Airport Industrial Estate in 1972. The aerodrome at Meir Heath ceased operations during the 1970s. During the war bomber aircraft were assembled at the aerodrome on what is now the site of the Creda Works.

1 The railway station and statue of Josiah Wedgwood are part of the only real attempt at a town plan in the 19th century in the Potteries. Fronted on one side by the station, and on the other by the *North Staffordshire Hotel*, the square presents an impressive welcome to the town for rail travellers. The station also reflects the importance attached to the rail network by the City's authorities.

2 View of Stoke from Penkhull by Henry Lark Pratt in about 1850. Even at this date Stoke and its neighbouring towns are still largely physically separated.

133 Campbell Place, Stoke-on-Trent. This inter-war view clearly shows the old National Provincial Bank building with its turret on the left. To the right of the photograph is the former Majestic Cinema which opened in 1914 on the site of the Campbell Works Potbank. Between 1924 and 1927 Radio Stoke-on-Trent, the first local radio station in the area, broadcast from the cinema. The Majestic closed in 1957.

134 Church Street, Stoke-on-Trent, in the 1920s or early 1930s. The *Ring o'Bells* public house stands to the left of the picture.

135 New recruits await embarkation from Stoke Station to training camps in about 1941. Many young local men served during the Second World War. Stoke station was an important transportation point in the movement of troops.

36 (*opposite above*) During the war, the City General Hospital suffered a hit. The newly completed nurses' home, rtunately not occupied at the time, suffered severe damage and access to wards and clinics was affected.

37 (*opposite below*) Bomb damage, May Bank. Stoke-on-Trent was not a high priority target for the Luftwaffe. Surplus ombs were dropped on the city by aircraft returning from Manchester and Liverpool. Surviving German maps indicated iority targets for raids, such as the hospital, railway station and sewage works.

38 (*above*) During the Second World War the ballroom at Trentham Gardens was used as a clearing bank. Many local omen were employed there; others served in the munitions factory at Swynnerton outside the city, and at Radway Green ear Alsager. A number of Stoke women joined the Land Army, while others served in further essential services such as e fire watch.

139 During the Second World War parks, grass verges, and other open spaces were turned over to growing vegetables. In Hanley Park members of the Women's Land Army maintained the grounds.

140 The Ionic columns of the Old Town Hall represented Hanley's civic pretensions before its administrative centre moved to the former *Queen's Hotel*. The Old Town Hall survived as a bank before it was finally demolished.

41 Aerial view of Hanley. The Bell Works, now the site of the City Museum and Art Gallery, are in the foreground; the Bethesda Chapel lies in the middle ground. A large proportion of the background now lies under the Potteries Shopping Centre.

142 A view of Pall Mall, Hanley, probably in the 1950s. The Theatre Royal is on the left and the horse and cart are already anachronistic.

143 Piccadilly, Hanley lies very close to the recent Potteries Shopping Centre development. Similar roads attract small local and often specialist businesses, and, despite the redevelopment around them, have changed very little.

44 The Diamond Jubilee of Queen Victoria was popularly celebrated in the Potteries. The new Bratt and Dykes epartment store opened in 1876 and is seen here bedecked with bunting for the Jubilee.

145 A posed photograph taken in the 1950s captures the unique quality of the Potteries. The image almost succeeds i presenting a romantic view of the potbank, but the overall cleanliness belies the reality.

146 Pollution of the air was a major problem in the Potteries. It caused respiratory diseases which were the major cause of death in the area at the turn of the century. Legislation to improve air-quality has been successful, and today, circulatory diseases and cancers account for the largest numbers of deaths in the area.

147 'Fresh air for the Potteries'. The irony of the title of this postcard cannot be lost, but it could almost be taken as slogan for the campaign to clean the air in the postwar era.

148 The nurses and patients of the Hartshill Children's Orthopaedic Hospital celebrated Christmas in 1925 as best they could in spartan surroundings. The holly sits uncomfortably amongst the moulds of the feet of children.

149 The Cottage Hospital, Longton, was originally opened in 1868. The present hospital dates from 1889-1890 and stands on land given by the Duke of Sutherland.

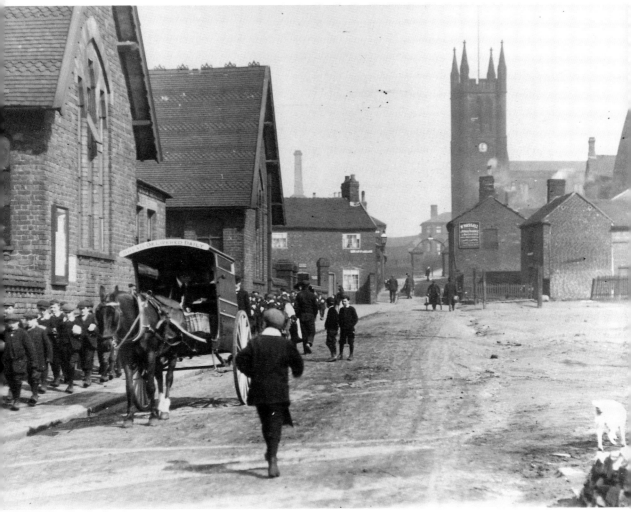

50   St James' School, Longton, *c.*1912. The proximity of housing, school, church and workplace is typical of industrialised
areas and indicates a pattern of life followed by generations of potters.

151 Longton railway station and bridge with St John's Church in the background. The area is now heavily congested with traffic. Longton is currently at the centre of a scheme of urban renewal, and has attracted investment from the European Community.

152 The original town hall in Longton was built in 1789 in Times Square and was replaced in 1863 by this building. It boasts a porte-cochère with giant Ionic columns beneath a pediment. An extension was added before the First World War.

153 In about 1892 Longton market boasted a pet supply stall which was run by Barkers. The Victorian demand for caged birds was great, as this photograph shows.

154 Market Street, Fenton. In comparison with Hanley, Fenton was a quiet town but was connected by tram services with its neighbours.

155 The National Westminster Bank occupied the former Athenaeum building in Fenton, which was demolished in 1977. It had been built to an Italianate design by Ward and Son of Hanley in 1853.

156 Fenton town hall was built in 1888, in a combination of late Gothic and Tudor styles of architecture. The architects were R. Scrivener and Sons of Hanley.

57 Siddall and Sons operated two general stores in Fenton around the turn of the century. General stores provided a local service to people before the arrival of supermarkets.

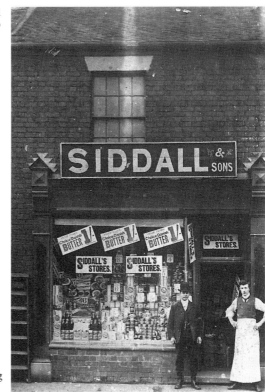

58 The warehouse of Siddall's in 1913 in a photograph illustrating the range of goods the company sold.

159 The First World War was brought to an official end with the Peace Treaty of 1919. Garden parties, such as this at Blurton House, were held to celebrate the event. The small rural community suffered many losses during the war and all the village turned out for the party.

160 (*above*) The Old Vicarage in Normacot, Longton. The Holy Evangelists' church in the background was built as a chapel of ease by the Duke of Sutherland in 1847 to a design by George Gilbert Scott.

161 (*right*) Caverswall village lies outside the city boundary and is best known for its castle. The oak tree once served as the nucleus of the village and was known as the town hall.

162 (*above*) Caverswall Castle. Licence to crenellate was given in 1275, and a house was built into the castle in about 1615.

163 The Cobridge Brick and Marl Company excavated raw materials on a large scale, as can be seen in this photograph of about 1929. The Sneyd Colliery is in the background.

164 *Carrying Out Ware* by C.W. Brown. Brown's paintings illustrated the pottery industry.